# GOING TO WAR IN
# ANCIENT
# GREECE

# ARMIES OF THE PAST

# GOING TO WAR IN
# ANCIENT
# GREECE

## ADRIAN GILBERT

## W
## FRANKLIN WATTS
### A Division of Grolier Publishing
NEW YORK • LONDON • HONG KONG • SYDNEY
DANBURY, CONNECTICUT

**ILLUSTRATIONS BY**
Mark Bergin
Giovanni Caselli
Chris Molan
Lee Montgomery
Peter Visscher
Maps by Stefan Chabluk

**Editor**  Penny Clarke
**Editor-in-Chief**  John C. Miles
**Designer**  Steve Prosser
**Art Director**  Jonathan Hair

First published in 2000 by
Franklin Watts
96 Leonard Street
London
EC2A 4XD

First American edition 2001 by Franklin Watts
A Division of Grolier Publishing
90 Sherman Turnpike
Danbury, CT 06816

Catalog details are available from the Library of
Congress Cataloging-in-Publication Data

Visit Franklin Watts on the internet at:
http://publishing.grolier.com

ISBN 0-531-14590-5 (lib.bdg)
    0-531-16351-2 (pbk)

Printed in Hong Kong/China

GROLIER
PUBLISHING

# CONTENTS

Greek settlements

Land battles

Sea battles

• Greek cities

MACEDONIA

Mt. Olympus

AEGEAN SEA

THESSALY

Thermopylae
BOEOTIA
Chaeronea    Athens
Leuctra    Thebes
Plataea    Marathon
Corinth    Piraeus
Salamis
Argos

PELOPONNESE
MESSENIA    Sparta
LACONIA

PAROS

ANCIENT GREECE

ADRIATIC SEA

Massilia

Neapolis

Syracuse

Syracuse 415 B.C.

# THE GREEK WORLD

The civilization that began to emerge in Greece from about 750 B.C. consisted of many city-states, the inhabitants of which all spoke the Greek language. Some city-states were little more than small towns and their surrounding land, but others, such as Athens and Sparta, became powerful. All had their own armies, and wars were frequent. Due to expanding populations and a shortage of good farmland, many Greeks left their homes to start up settlements in other lands.

Kinyps

TRIPOLIS

*Late 8th-century B.C. armor from Argos, the earliest complete Greek armor*

### Origins 1200 B.C.
The early Greek Mycenaean civilization is overthrown. Greece enters a "dark age" until around 750 B.C., when a new Greek culture emerges.

### City-states 750-650 B.C.
Rival Greek-speaking city-states emerge. Each has its own army.

### Persian invasions 490-479 B.C.
Greece is invaded by Persia in 490 B.C. and again in 480 B.C. On both occasions the Greeks defeat the Persians and force them to withdraw.

Battles:
A. *Thermopylae 480 B.C.*
B. *Leuctra 371 B.C.*
   *Plataea 479 B.C.*
   *Chaeronea 338 B.C.*
C. *Marathon 490 B.C.*

Tanais

Olbia

Istrus

BLACK SEA

Odessus

THRACE

Apollonia

MACEDONIA

Byzantium

Phasis

Trapezus

THESSALY   AEGEAN
           SEA          Phocea

A.

B.

C.

SAMOS

Athens

Miletus

Sparta

*Salamis 480 B.C.*

RHODES

*Siege of Rhodes 305-304 B.C.*

CRETE

CYPRUS

Cyrene

Naucratis

### Rise of Macedonia
### 340-335 B.C.
Under the leadership of
Philip II and his son
Alexander, Macedonia
dominates the Greek city-
states.

### Campaigns of Alexander
### 334-323 B.C.
Alexander defeats the
Persians and creates a
new Greek empire in Asia.
He leads his army as far
as India.

*The Parthenon, the temple
of Athena, built on the
Acropolis in Athens
between 447 and 438 B.C.*

EGYPT

RED SEA

*Bronze
statuette of
a Spartan
warrior*

### Athens
### triumphant 479-431 B.C.
The dynamic city-state of Athens
enters a golden period of good,
settled government. Art, literature,
and the theater flourish.

### The Peloponnesian
### War 431-404 B.C.
War breaks out between
Athens and other city-states
led by Sparta. After nearly
30 years, Athens is defeated.

### Battle of
### Leuctra 371 B.C.
The Spartans are beaten by
a Theban army at Leuctra.
The Thebans use new tactics
to overcome the Spartans.

# SOLDIERS OF THE CITY-STATE

Greek city-states adopted similar ways of waging war. Around the 7th century B.C., cavalry, which had been an important part of earlier Greek armies, was replaced by heavily armed infantry called *hoplites*.

Athens, the largest of the city-states, had a huge army at the height of its power. The Athenians elected ten generals (*strategoi*) who helped govern the state in peacetime and lead the army in war. If a general displeased the people, he could be dismissed and punished.

## WARFARE AND FARMING

In ancient Greece, warfare and agriculture were closely linked. Military campaigns usually did not last long so that soldiers could return to their farms at harvest time.

Military writers believed that good farmers made good warriors. On becoming a soldier, a hoplite swore an oath to defend "the wheat, the barley, the vines, the olives, and the figs."

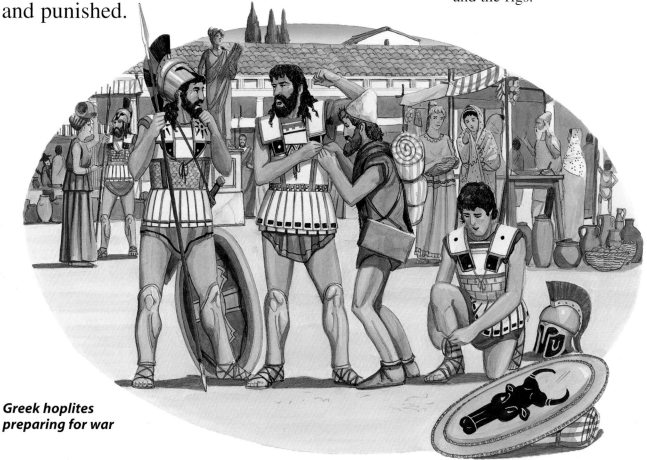

*Greek hoplites preparing for war*

## PREPARING FOR WAR

In time of war, all male citizens of Athens over the age of 17 were required to serve as soldiers. Hoplites were mainly recruited from farmers.

These men were wealthy enough to supply their own armor and weapons.

# FAMOUS COMMANDERS

**PERICLES (495–429 B.C.)**
A great statesman and general, Pericles played a major role in the expansion of Athenian power in the 5th century B.C. He supervised the rebuilding of the Acropolis.

**ALEXANDER THE GREAT (356–323 B.C.)**
A supremely gifted soldier, Alexander united the Greeks under his command. In less than a decade he conquered the Persian Empire.

Unlike the elected generals of Athens, Alexander had total power over his army and was ruthless in imposing his will.

**MILITIADES (550–489 B.C.)**
Militiades defeated the Persians at the battle of Marathon (490 B.C.). But after failing to capture the island of Paros, he returned to Athens in disgrace and was fined.

ΡΕΡΙΚΛΗΣ

## WARRIORS ALL

Greeks from all occupations regarded military service as a great honor. Although he was short and pot-bellied, the philosopher Socrates (469–399 B.C.) fought with great bravery as a hoplite.

The playwright Sophocles (496–406 B.C.) was a distinguished naval commander, while the author and dramatist Aeschylus (525–456 B.C.) fought the Persians at Marathon, where his brother was killed.

## THE PRICE OF COMMAND

Athenian generals could find themselves harshly treated by their own people. After the naval battle of Arginusae in 406 B.C., eight commanders were sentenced to death because they had not rescued Athenian sailors who had fallen in the water.

Socrates tried to stop the sentence from being carried out, but all eight were executed by the vengeful citizens.

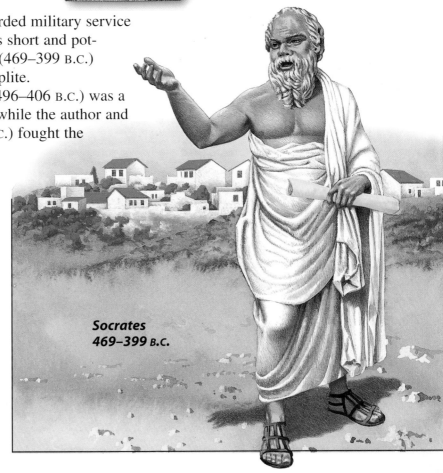

*Socrates
469–399 B.C.*

# SPARTA

The Spartans were a Greek people who lived in the Peloponnese (the southernmost part of Greece). In the 8th century B.C. they conquered the neighboring state of Messenia, enslaving its people. A series of wars with Argos and a revolt by the Messenians in 630 B.C. led Sparta to develop a unique military society to protect its territory.

Only Spartan-born males could become citizens, and all had to join the army. They were not allowed to do any other work, and spent all their time training for war. Sparta had two kings who acted as generals in war, although real power lay in the hands of the five magistrates (*ephors*).

### THE WAY OF THE WARRIOR

All Spartan men had to live in barracks with their fellow soldiers until old age. They were not allowed to marry until the age of 30, and even then a soldier was only allowed to visit his wife and family at intervals.

Other city-states both respected and feared the Spartans' bravery and fighting skills.

*A Spartan soldier ready for battle wears his red cloak and bronze cuirass (torso armor).*

The Spartans were the most feared warriors in Greece. The writer and philosopher Plutarch noted that they:

*"Marched in step to the pipe, leaving no confusion in their hearts, but calmly and cheerfully advanced into danger."*

### SPARTAN TROOPS

Spartan soldiers were equipped with armor and weapons in the same way as the soldiers of other Greek armies, although their red tunics and cloaks made them stand out on the battlefield.

Spartan soldiers were also distinguished by their long hair, which they carefully combed before battle.

*Stone bust of King Leonidas*

## 🔶 THE PERSIAN INVASION

In 480 B.C. a vast Persian army commanded by the emperor Xerxes invaded Greece. A small force of Spartans led by King Leonidas was annihilated while trying to defend a mountainous pass at Thermopylae.

## 🔶 RESISTANCE

As Spartans, it was unthinkable for Leonidas and his men to flee before the relentless onslaught of the Persians at Thermopylae. However, their brave stand was not wasted, as it encouraged the other Greek city-states to fight and finally defeat the Persians.

After Thermopylae, the invaders marched south and captured Athens, but were defeated at the naval battle of Salamis. The following year, 479 B.C., the Persians were decisively beaten on land at the battle of Plataea and were driven from Greece.

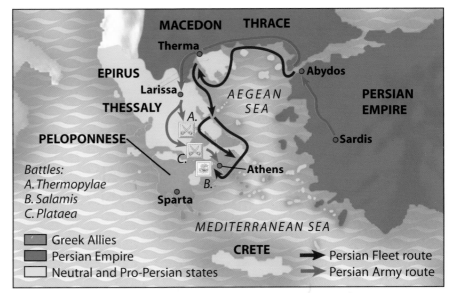

Map labels: MACEDON, THRACE, Therma, EPIRUS, Abydos, Larissa, THESSALY, AEGEAN SEA, PERSIAN EMPIRE, PELOPONNESE, A., Sardis, C., Athens, B., Sparta, MEDITERRANEAN SEA, CRETE

Battles:
A. Thermopylae
B. Salamis
C. Plataea

Greek Allies
Persian Empire
Neutral and Pro-Persian states
→ Persian Fleet route
→ Persian Army route

# HARD LIVES

## SPARTAN BOYS

At the age of seven, boys were taken from their mothers and sent to schools that emphasized discipline and exercise. Conditions were harsh to prepare them for war.

## SPARTAN GIRLS

Spartan girls, unlike girls in the rest of Greece, were encouraged to exercise and compete in athletic events.

It was hoped that this would make them fitter and stronger mothers, who would give birth to more and healthier children.

## HELOTS

The people captured by the Spartans were called helots. They worked as slaves, farming the land. The Spartans were always fearful of helot rebellion, and during peacetime the army kept the helots in order.

# THE HOPLITE

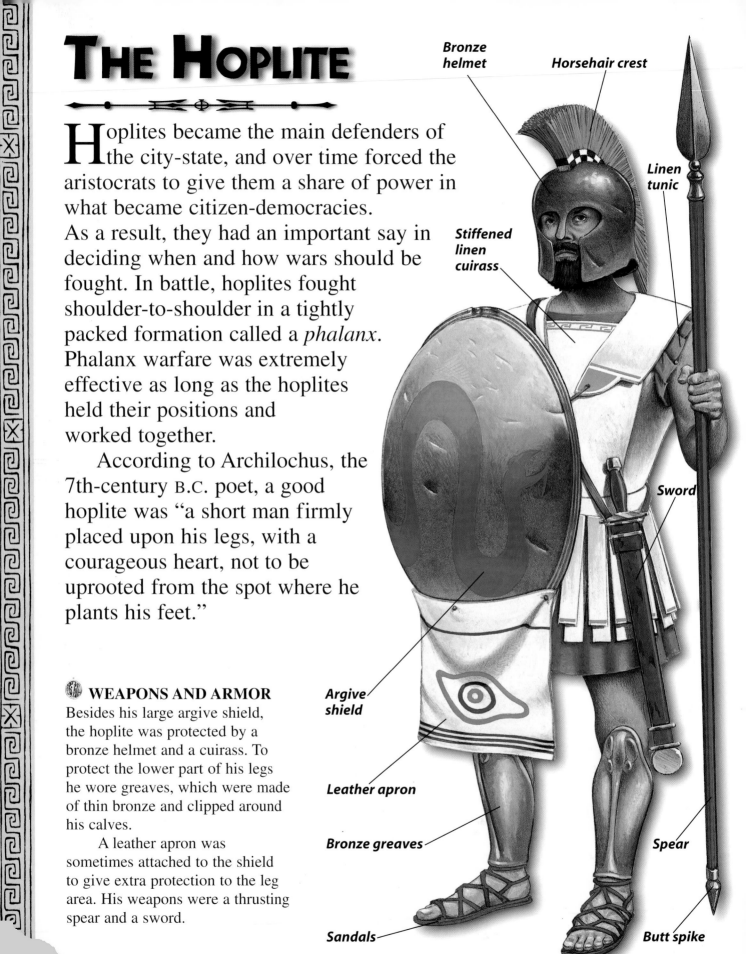

Hoplites became the main defenders of the city-state, and over time forced the aristocrats to give them a share of power in what became citizen-democracies. As a result, they had an important say in deciding when and how wars should be fought. In battle, hoplites fought shoulder-to-shoulder in a tightly packed formation called a *phalanx*. Phalanx warfare was extremely effective as long as the hoplites held their positions and worked together.

According to Archilochus, the 7th-century B.C. poet, a good hoplite was "a short man firmly placed upon his legs, with a courageous heart, not to be uprooted from the spot where he plants his feet."

### WEAPONS AND ARMOR

Besides his large argive shield, the hoplite was protected by a bronze helmet and a cuirass. To protect the lower part of his legs he wore greaves, which were made of thin bronze and clipped around his calves.

A leather apron was sometimes attached to the shield to give extra protection to the leg area. His weapons were a thrusting spear and a sword.

Bronze helmet

Horsehair crest

Linen tunic

Stiffened linen cuirass

Sword

Argive shield

Leather apron

Bronze greaves

Spear

Sandals

Butt spike

# WEAPONS

## SHIELDS
Hoplite shields were a symbol of courage, and to throw one away in battle was a disgrace. Spartan women told their soldiers to return either with their shields or on them.

## SWORDS
Hoplites only used their short iron swords if their spears were broken or for fighting at close range.

*Hoplite sword*

*Hoplite spear*

## SPEARS
Spears were the hoplites' principal weapon. The shaft was made from a strong wood such as ash, and besides the iron spear-head it had a bronze butt spike. This was used to stab men who had fallen to the ground during the battle.

*Bronze cuirass*

## A HEAVY BURDEN
The weapons and armor carried and worn by the hoplites were very heavy. The 1/4-inch (6-millimeter)-thick cuirass could weigh up to 30 pounds (13.5 kilograms) and the shield added another 20 pounds (9 kilograms).

Overall, the hoplite's armor amounted to about half his body weight. As a result, hoplites could not move very fast and tended to favor simple defensive tactics.

## ARMOR
The cuirass, which protected the chest and back, was made up of two plates joined together at the sides. Heavy bronze cuirasses (often shaped with the muscles of the torso) were popular among hoplite officers, although leather and stiffened linen were also common.

Shields were made from thick strips of oak, covered with leather or bronze.

*Back of a hoplite's shield showing holding straps*

*Corinthian helmet*

## HELMET DESIGN
The Corinthian helmet, which covered much of the wearer's face, was very popular in the 6th and 5th centuries B.C. It was very heavy, but provided excellent protection.

An elaborate horsehair crest was attached to the crown of the helmet as a means of identification — and to make its wearer look more impressive.

# CAVALRY AND SKIRMISHERS

The packed phalanx of hoplites dominated Greek warfare for more than 200 years, but during the 5th century B.C. — as a result of the Persian Wars (490–479 B.C.) and the Peloponnesian War (431–404 B.C.) — tactics began to change, and cavalry became important.

The phalanx was effective on flat, open ground but not in hills and rough country. Those areas suited lightly armed troops. Cavalry went on scouting missions and hunted down fleeing enemy infantrymen, while skirmishers (lightly armed foot soldiers) harassed the enemy's phalanx before the main battle.

**Lightly armed cavalryman**

The Athenian commander Iphicrates believed that armies would be more effective if cavalry and light troops fought alongside the hoplite phalanx:

*"The light-armed troops are like the hands, the cavalry like the feet, the line of men-at-arms like chest and breastplate, and the general like the head."*

## CAVALRY

Cavalrymen normally came from wealthy families because buying and keeping horses was an expensive business.

The best cavalry came from the northern Greek state of Thessaly. For centuries, the grazing land for which the state was famous had led to the breeding of fine horses, and a tradition of outstanding horsemanship had developed.

## WEAPONS

Cavalrymen rode their horses without stirrups and usually bareback. They rarely wore armor and their weapons consisted of a couple of javelins and a sword.

When fighting against hoplites, cavalry threw their javelins at the enemy soldiers and then retreated to safety. They were not expected to take on the phalanx in hand-to-hand combat.

## LIGHT TROOPS

*Psiloi* and *gymnets* were two groups of lightly armed Greek skirmishers. In addition, there were the *peltasts* who were recruited from Thrace and harried the enemy phalanx.

The Athenians used Scythian archers, although the best bowmen came from Crete. The island of Rhodes was famous as a source of slingers.

### PSILOI
These troops wielded a club and threw stones to harass the enemy.

### GYMNETS
Equipped only with swords, gymnets were of little use in a major phalanx battle.

### ARCHERS
Archers with powerful bows provided long-range firepower to support the phalanx.

### SLINGERS
Slingers fired stones at the enemy with considerable accuracy.

### PELTASTS
Armed with javelins, Thracian peltasts carried a distinctive crescent-shaped shield.

# SLINGSHOTS AND BOWS

*Slingshot*

*Shot*

*Strung bow*

*Unstrung bow*

*Strung bow ready to fire*

### SLINGSHOTS
Hurled from a leather sling, shot was made from small stones, clay, or lead. Sometimes the slinger inscribed messages onto his shot, such as "Take that!"

### COMPOSITE BOWS
Composite bows, which were made from a combination of wood, horn, bone, and animal tendons, were strong and could fire arrows a long way with great accuracy.

### DRAWING THE BOW
The most powerful composite bows — used by Scythian archers — were very difficult to draw back, so archers had to be extremely strong.

# THE SHOCK OF BATTLE

Early Greek civilizations had fought each other in small groups, but from around 750 B.C. onward, city-states began to organize their soldiers to fight in phalanxes. Battles in which one phalanx fought another became the standard form of confrontation in Greek warfare over the next four centuries.

The two sides would normally agree on the site of a battle by picking a flat piece of land on which the phalanx could move easily. After sacrifices to the gods, the two armies lined up facing each other. Then the order to attack would be given, and the two great masses of shields and spears crashed into each other.

BOEOTIA
Leuctra • • Thebes
*Battle of Leuctra 371 B.C.* ⚔ • Athens
PELOPONNESE
MESSENIA
• Sparta
LACONIA MEDITERRANEAN SEA

### BATTLE OF LEUCTRA
In 371 B.C. Epaminondas's Theban army defeated a more powerful Spartan force using new tactics. The enemy's right wing was overwhelmed, and the Spartan king and all his best troops were killed.

## BATTLE TACTICS

### PHALANX AT WORK
The phalanx could be several hundred men across and usually anything from eight to 16 men deep. The first three ranks stabbed at their opponents with their spears. Ranks behind tried to push them forward to break the enemy line.

### INTERLOCKING SHIELDS
Within the phalanx, each hoplite's shield partly protected him and the man on his right. In battle, the phalanx tended to move to the right as each man sought protection from his neighbor's shield.

Spartans

Thebans

### THEBAN TACTICS
At Leuctra, Thebans used large numbers of light troops and massed their hoplites into a 50-deep phalanx on their left wing, while their center and right wing hung back. The 12-deep Spartan phalanx could not withstand the Thebans' charge.

## CLASH OF SHIELDS

Success in a typical hoplite battle depended upon raw courage and brute strength. Once the two sides were locked in battle, the side that pushed forward and broke into the enemy phalanx won the battle. Each hoplite tried to stab the vulnerable and unprotected parts of his opponents while trying to protect himself with his own shield. Hoplites who fell during the fighting were trampled underfoot and stabbed with swords or the butt spikes of the spears of their enemies. The fighting was bloody, vicious, and terrifying.

*The auloi, or double pipes*

## MARCHING TO MUSIC

The phalanx was accompanied by musicians playing horns and double-piped instruments called *auloi*. While the music encouraged the hoplites to fight (and frightened the enemy), it also helped the soldiers keep in step as they marched. Keeping in step was important in the closely packed phalanx formation.

*Greek musician playing the auloi*

*Combat between phalanxes was a very bloody business. The Greek soldier and historian Xenophon described the battlefield after the second Battle of Coronea in 394 B.C.:*

*"The earth was stained in blood, and the remains of friends and enemies lay side-by-side. There were shattered shields, broken spears, and unsheathed swords, some lying about on the ground, others stuck in corpses, and others still gripped as if to strike even in death."*

# SIEGE WARFARE

Until the Peloponnesian War (431–404 B.C.), the Greeks had rarely besieged each other's cities. Battles were fought in the open — protected by their walls, cities were usually safe, unless defeated by starvation or treachery.

Among the changes that took place in Greek warfare in the 5th century B.C. were the development of siege weapons and special techniques to break down city walls. Sieges became more common; defenders increased the strength of city walls, and attackers invented more powerful siege weapons.

## SIEGE IN PROGRESS

Breaking down the city's walls became the key objective of a besieging army (below). Tunnelers burrowed underground to weaken foundations, and battering rams smashed their way through at weak points.

Siege artillery — crossbows and catapults — fired missiles, while archers shot at enemy troops manning the walls. Later, armored siege towers might be rolled into place to allow the attackers to get over the walls and enter the city.

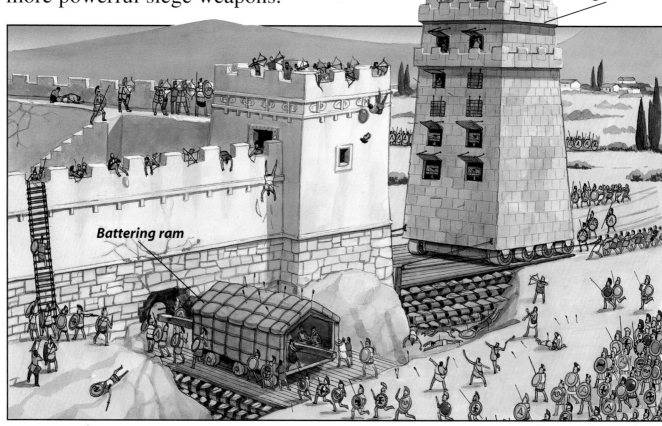

*Siege tower*

*Battering ram*

## THE THEORY OF SIEGES

During the 4th century B.C. many military writers produced manuals about siege warfare. Dionysius I of Syracuse (a Greek colony in Sicily) used the latest siege machinery — including catapults and towers — during his successful assault on Moyta in 397 B.C. His ideas influenced the Macedonians, who became masters of siege warfare under Philip II and Alexander.

# SIEGE WEAPONS

### Catapult

### CROSSBOW

Siege crossbows operated like ordinary bows, but because the bow was so large and stiff, the string had to be pulled back using a winch. Crossbows were also used by soldiers on the city walls to fire at siege equipment such as battering rams and siege towers.

*Crossbow*

*Battering ram*

### BATTERING RAM

A battering ram consisted of a tree trunk with a metal point on one end suspended from a wheeled frame. When swung, the ram smashed through weak points in the walls. The soldiers operating the ram were protected from enemy arrows by the hide-covered roof and sides.

### CATAPULT

This type of stone-firing catapult was used by Alexander at the siege of Tyre (332 B.C.). Each arm of the catapult was held in place by tightly twisted cords or horse hair, which provided the power to fire the projectile.

## PELOPONNESIAN WAR

The rivalry between Athens and Sparta and their many allies burst into open warfare in 431 B.C. The turning point of the war was the Athenians' siege of Syracuse in 415 B.C. (below).

Helped by the Spartans, the garrison of Syracuse held out, defeating first the Athenian navy and then destroying their army.

## THE CITY-TAKER

During the siege of Rhodes in 305–304 B.C., the attackers constructed an enormous siege tower. Protected by iron plates, it was called a city-taker, or *helepolis* (right).

The tower, which is thought to have been 138 feet (42 meters) high, had catapults inside. Fortunately for the people of Rhodes, it proved ineffective.

*Wheels rolled tower forward*

- Neutral States
- Allies of Athens
- Allies of Sparta in Sicily
- The Spartan Confederacy
- Athens and the Delian League

Byzantium
Potidea
Athens
Sparta
PERSIAN EMPIRE
IONIA
SICILY
Syracuse
RHODES
CRETE

# WAR AT SEA

Greek shipbuilding was influenced by the Phoenicians, a seafaring people who lived around the eastern and southern shores of the Mediterranean.

The first Greek warships, or *penteconters*, had 50 oarsmen seated in a row. In the 8th century B.C. the Greeks copied the Phoenicians' *bireme*, with two rows of oars. This developed into the *trireme* (three rows of oars) in the 5th century B.C. Later, even larger ships were built.

Athens had a long history of sea trade, and after the battle of Salamis (480 B.C.) it built up a powerful navy. This helped Athens acquire a large empire in and around the Aegean Sea, although this caused much resentment among other Greek city-states.

The Athenian navy was very expensive and needed large numbers of rowers – over 20,000 men on one occasion. Rowers were recruited from free men who could not afford to buy the armor and weapons needed by hoplites.

**Large single sail**

**Banks of rowers**

## THE TRIREME

Triremes (above) were about 130 feet (40 meters) long and had a crew of around 200: 170 rowers and 30 crewmen and marines. Triremes usually sailed within sight of land; in the evenings, the ships were beached and the crew spent the night on shore. Before a battle, the sails and rigging were taken down, and the trireme was propelled entirely by its rowers.

## THE BATTLE OF SALAMIS

**Greek naval base**

**ATTICA**

**Battle of Salamis 480 B.C.**

**Athens**

**Piraeus**

**Salamis**

*Persian fleet forms a blockade here*

**SALAMIS**

MEDITERRANEAN SEA

→ Route of Persian fleets
→ Greek fleet retreats then attacks

## BATTLE OF SALAMIS 480 B.C.

During the second Persian invasion, a fleet of 200 Greek triremes faced 800 Persian ships. The Greeks withdrew to the narrow channels around the island of Salamis so that the Persians had no room to maneuver.

When the Greeks attacked, their fighting and rowing skills forced the Persians to retreat. After this defeat, the Persians began to withdraw from Greece.

## BRONZE RAM

The prow, or front, of the trireme was made of bronze and rammed enemy ships. The rowers propelled the trireme fast enough for the ram to pierce the enemy's hull.

Many Greek ships had an eye painted near the prow to ward off the "evil eye" — a motif that is still seen on Greek boats today.

*The bronze prow of the trireme smashed into enemy ships.*

## BATTLE TACTICS

### RAM AHEAD

The usual tactic was for the attacking ship to ram the middle of the enemy vessel. If this was successful, the enemy ship would be so badly damaged that it would sink within a matter of minutes.

### ROWING A TRIREME

Oars were arranged in three rows with a man to each oar. For short periods the rowers could propel their trireme through the water at speeds of up to 10 mph (16 km/h) — very fast for human power.

### ATTACK FROM THE SIDE

A complex tactic was that in which a trireme went alongside an enemy ship, pulling in its own oars as it did so and smashing those of the enemy. The disabled ship was now vulnerable to boarding or ramming.

# AN ARMY ON THE MOVE

Hoplite armies always needed large numbers of civilians to help transport soldiers' weapons and gear. In addition to servants and slaves carrying baggage on foot, mules, horses, and carts were used to move heavy equipment.

While on the march, hoplites normally ate barley, which was ground up and mixed into a porridge. If food was plentiful they might eat cheese, salted meat, and onions. And at certain times of the year they would be able to scavenge local produce, such as figs and olives.

## PREPARING THE WAY

In the Spartan army, men who had been rejected as not good enough to become hoplites were used to clear the way for the baggage carts and other heavy equipment.

They were given shovels, axes, and sickles, and they played an important role in making sure the army could move to the battlefield with as little delay as possible.

**Packhorse**

**Cavalry trooper**

**Servant**

**Foot soldier**

## CAMP FOLLOWERS

When an army went on a long campaign, it took with it craftsmen to help repair arms and equipment damaged in battle or in transit. These included blacksmiths, carpenters, and leather workers. Other civilians, or camp followers, included the hoplites' servants, women, and even children. Sometimes so many camp followers accompanied the army that it became very slow and cumbersome. Commanders tried to limit the number of camp followers, but seldom with much success.

## ✦ BATTLE PREPARATIONS

Getting ready for battle was an elaborate business for a hoplite. This is shown on the left in this vase painting. He combed and tidied his hair before putting on the heavy Corinthian helmet. The cuirass came next, followed by the greaves on his legs.

Putting on his armor properly was important, for every hoplite knew that in a few hours he might be either a victor or among the vanquished dead.

*Vase painting (500 B.C.) of hoplites arming for battle*

## ✦ SERVANTS AND SLAVES

Each Spartan hoplite had a helot to carry his weapons and armor. An Athenian hoplite used one of the slaves or servants who worked on his farm.

Slaves and servants also prepared food and built shelters. Before battle, they cleaned and prepared their masters' weapons. Great care was taken of shields, which had an almost religious importance for the warriors.

*A servant packs a shield in its leather cover.*

## ✦ MEDICAL AID

Although the Greeks had only very limited knowledge of how the body worked, attempts were made to help wounded and injured men. Philip II employed surgeons in his army, and they operated on soldiers injured in battle. There were no anesthetics. If his wounds became infected, a soldier would almost certainly die.

*Greek surgical instruments*

# WAR AND THE GODS

The Greeks worshiped many gods and believed that they must have their approval if they were to be successful in battle. And yet, while the Greeks thought that wars were inevitable, they did not always consider them a good thing.

Many writers described the damage and suffering caused by conflicts. The Theban poet Pindar warned that war "was a sweet thing to him that does not know it, but to him who has made a trial of it, it is a thing of fear."

## SACRIFICE

Before battle, a commander would order the sacrifice of a goat or a sheep. It was hoped that the sacrifice would please the gods and bring victory.

## GODS

### ARES
The god of war, Ares was violent and short-tempered. According to the poet Homer, Zeus said: "To me you are the most hateful of all the gods who hold Olympus."

### ATHENA
The patron of Athens, Athena was also the goddess of wisdom and war. She was often shown wearing hoplite armor and carrying weapons.

### NIKE
*Nike* was the Greek word for "victory," and was usually personified as a beautiful winged goddess, sometimes carrying a spear and a shield. Statues of Nike were common throughout Greece.

The experienced naval commander and playwright Sophocles condemned war in these lines from his famous tragedy Ajax:

"Whoever it was that first revealed to Greece ubiquitous war with its hateful arms, I curse him! Generations of suffering he wrought, for he was a destroyer of men."

## SOPHOCLES

As well as being a great playwright, Sophocles (c.496–406 B.C.) was a naval commander who played a leading role in the capture of Samos. Like many other Greek writers and artists, he had practical experience of war and wrote about it in his plays.

*A victorious hoplite - bound by the nomima*

## PRISONERS

Until the Peloponnesian War, the city-states would normally swap their prisoners after a battle. But the old rules of war were largely ignored in this brutal conflict, and prisoners were often slaughtered by their captors.

At the end of one battle during the war, Philocles, the victorious Athenian admiral, ordered that the crews from two captured triremes should be thrown off a cliff.

*A Spartan hoplite prepares to kill a prisoner.*

## RULES OF WAR

The hoplite (left) represented what was best in the city-state: an honest farmer brave in battle and generous in victory. He was theoretically bound by the rules of war called the *nomima*. This included fair treatment of prisoners.

# THE ARMY OF MACEDONIA

The northern state of Macedonia played little part in Greek affairs until Philip II became king in 359 B.C. He built up a strong army and began to expand his territories by conquest, first to the east and then south toward the Greek heartland.

The other Greek city-states opposed Macedonian expansion, but they did not band together to fight Philip until it was too late. In 338 B.C., at the battle of Chaeronea, the forces of the city-states were decisively defeated, and Philip became master of Greece.

Macedonian pikemen advancing in a phalanx was awe inspiring. One writer explained how Aemilius Paulus, a Roman commander who fought the Macedonians, remembered his fear on seeing the enemy:

"He considered the formidable appearance of their front, bristling with arms, and was taken with fear and alarm: nothing he had ever seen before was its equal."

## THE MACEDONIAN PHALANX

Unlike the Greek phalanx, which depended on soldiers forming a defensive wall, the Macedonian phalanx relied on offense to defeat the enemy (above). Armor was lighter and the soldiers' spears (*sarissas*) much longer. This meant that from the first five ranks of the Macedonian phalanx, spear points projected at the enemy.

## PHILIP'S ARMY

The phalanx was central to the success of the Macedonian army, but Philip also used lightly armed troops. He introduced a new type of infantry called *hypaspists*. Armed with swords and short spears, they protected the flanks of the phalanx. Unlike the Greek city-states, Macedonia was ruled by a king with his aristocratic followers (called Companions), most of whom fought as mounted soldiers. As a result, cavalry was very important in the Macedonian army.

*The phalangite's spear was up to 20 ft (6 m) in length.*

## THE PHALANGITE

The soldiers of the Macedonian phalanx were called *phalangites*. They were lightly equipped with a simple helmet and light armor, and because they needed both hands to hold the sarissa, they wore their small shield slung over their shoulder by a leather strap. The phalangites were highly disciplined and underwent rugged training involving long marches carrying their equipment.

# MACEDONIA

*Ivory carving of Philip II*

### PHILIP II

Philip (*c*.382–336 B.C.) was a fine trainer of soldiers and a skillful general who combined light and heavy infantry with cavalry to outmaneuver his slower opponents.

### NEW HELMETS

The Macedonian army used different helmets from those worn by Athenian hoplites in the 5th century B.C. and earlier. The Thracian helmet covered less of the wearer's face, enabling him to see and hear better.

*Thracian helmet*

Cavalry and hypaspists
Phalanx
Peltasts

### MACEDONIAN TACTICS

Peltasts and other light troops would soften up the enemy with missile attacks. They would then retire behind the main phalanx, which was supported on the flanks by cavalry and hypaspists.

# ALEXANDER THE GREAT

Alexander the Great benefited from inheriting the combined Macedonian/Greek army built up by his father Philip, and used it to go campaigning in the east.

Intensely ambitious, Alexander always tried to destroy an enemy army as a first step to seizing new territory. Once the Persian Empire had been overthrown, he incorporated Persian troops in his army to allow him to continue his advance. Only the refusal of Alexander's soldiers to follow him into India halted his career of conquest.

*Bust of Alexander the Great*

## ALEXANDER
Succeeding to the throne in 336 B.C., the 20-year-old Alexander (above) immediately began an invasion of the Persian empire.

Over the next 13 years he engaged in almost constant warfare, dying of exhaustion and fever in Babylon in 323 B.C. Although brave, Alexander could also be very cruel, killing anyone who displeased him.

## COMPANIONS
The eight squadrons of mounted troops known as the Companions were the elite troops of Alexander's army. They were recruited from the Macedonian aristocracy.

The Companions were more heavily equipped than traditional Greek cavalry and carried a long thrusting spear. They did not skirmish before the main infantry battle but, arranged in a wedge-shaped formation, charged directly at the enemy.

*One of Alexander's Companions*

## THE CONQUESTS OF ALEXANDER

**MACEDONIA**

BLACK SEA

CASPIAN SEA

Pella

*River Granicus 334 B.C.*

Athens

*Issus 333 B.C.*

Miletus

*Gaugamela 331 B.C.*

Tashkent

Bukhara

*Hydaspes 326 B.C.*

Susia

Bactra

MEDITERRANEAN SEA

Ecbatana

Alexandria Areion (Herat)

Bucephala

*Tyre 332 B.C.*

Alexandria

Kandahar

Babylon (Death of Alexander 323 B.C.)

Susa

Memphis

**EGYPT**

RED SEA

Persepolis

Alexandria (Gulashkird)

Alexandria

ARABIAN SEA

- ☐ Alexander's empire
- ⚔ Major battles
- → Route of Alexander

## ALEXANDER'S EMPIRE

Alexander defeated the Persians in Asia Minor at Granicus and Issus before conquering Egypt. He then led his forces into Persia, destroying the Persian army at Gaugamela. Although he defeated an Indian army at Hydaspes, his exhausted troops refused to go farther, forcing Alexander to return to Persia.

*Alexander was a brilliant speaker, inspiring his troops to fight harder in battle. This is part of his speech to the army before the Battle of Issus (333 B.C.):*

*"We Macedonians are to fight Medes and Persians, nations long steeped in luxury, while we have long been hardened by warlike toils and dangers; and above all it will be a fight of free men against slaves."*

## ELEPHANTS

At the battle of Hydaspes, Alexander saw elephants for the first time. He then began using them in his own armies, adding fighting "castles" for archers and spearmen.

After Alexander's death, elephants were widely used by the Greek generals who succeeded him — many were brought back to Greece from India.

**Greek war elephant ready for battle**

29

# GLOSSARY

**Dates in ancient Greece are dated backward from the birth of Christ (B.C.). Centuries are listed below.**

First century = 1–99 B.C.
Second century = 100–199 B.C.
Third century = 200–299 B.C.
Fourth century = 300–399 B.C.
Fifth century = 400–499 B.C.
Sixth century = 500–599 B.C.
Seventh century = 600–699 B.C.

*Piper playing the auloi*

**Argive shield**
Round concave shield used by hoplites.

**Aristocratic**
People of the highest class who belonged to the powerful land-owning families. From the Greek word *aristoi*, "the best people."

**Auloi**
The double pipes that accompanied soldiers into battle. They were fitted with reeds and are thought to have made a sound a little like the modern oboe.

**Campaign**
The period when an army marched away to fight an enemy.

**Citizen**
A free adult male within the city-state. He was given the right to vote but was also expected to fight if the state became involved in a war.

**Cuirass**
Armor consisting of a breastplate and backplate to protect the soldier's torso. The cuirass could be made from a variety of materials, including bronze, leather, and stiffened linen.

**Democracy**
The political system that operated in many Greek city-states, especially Athens. In democratic states, citizens were given a say in how the city was run. This included the right to vote.

**Helots**
People captured by the Spartans who were treated like slaves. They were forced to work on Sparta's farms so Spartan men could concentrate on training to become soldiers.

**Hoplite**
Heavily armored Greek foot soldier. The name is thought to derive from the word *hopla*, meaning the weapons and equipment that had to be carried by the soldier.

**Bust of Pericles**

ΡΕΡΙΚΛΗΣ

### Hypaspist

Soldier in the Macedonian army who was more lightly armed and equipped than the hoplite and who fought between the cavalry and the phalangites of the main phalanx. The word means "shield bearer."

### Javelin

Short spear used mainly for throwing at the enemy.

### Marine

Soldier who operated on board a ship and was trained in ship-to-ship fighting.

### Nomima

Code of conduct that encouraged soldiers to treat others fairly, especially prisoners.

### Non-combatant

Person involved in a war who was not a soldier. This included people such as musicians and surgeons.

### Peloponnese

The southernmost part of Greece, linked to the rest of the country by the strip of land known as the Isthmus of Corinth. The area was inhabited by the Dorian tribes and included the city-states of Sparta and Corinth.

### Peltast

Lightly armed soldier, originating from the northern state of Thrace. Peltasts became common in Greek armies from the end of the 5th century B.C. onward. The name is derived from the word *pelte*, referring to the distinctive curved shields carried by Thracian peltasts.

### Phalangite

Macedonian soldier who wore little armor but was armed with a long spear (*sarissa*) and fought within the phalanx.

### Phalanx

Tightly packed formation of infantrymen armed with spears, made up of either hoplites or Macedonian phalangites. The phalanx was typically anything from eight to 16 ranks deep, although the Thebans sometimes deployed a phalanx that was up to 50 ranks deep.

### Skirmishing

Form of fighting by lightly armed and equipped soldiers, operating individually in the open.

*The helepolis: the Greeks' iron-clad siege tower*

# INDEX